알파 영어

벳만 알고 시작하는

정답 및 해석

Practice 1

1	we	11	he
2	we	12	she
3	you	13	you
4	they	14	we
5	those	15	we
6	you	16	they
7	these	17	you
8	he	18	he
9	I	19	it
10	she	20	you

Practice 3

43	I'm	54	He's
44	He's	55	They're
45	We're	56	It's
46	She's	57	It's
47	You're	58	They're
48	You're	59	This is
49	She's	60	This is
50	I'm	61	These are
51	We're	62	That's
52	She's	63	That's
53	He's	64	Those are

Practice 2

21	am	32	is
22	is	33	are
23	are	34	is
24	is	35	is
25	are	36	are
26	are	37	is
27	is	38	is
28	is	39	are
29	are	40	is
30	Is	41	is
31	is	42	are

Practice 4

65	My	78	My
66	our	79	Their
67	Her	80	my mother's
68	Sally's	81	Mark's
69	my sister's	82	June's
70	His	83	their
71	Jack's	84	Sally's
72	our	85	Sam's
73	Her	86	their
74	Her uncle's	87	sister's
75	my mother's	88	hers
76	His, Sam's	89	my
77	Sam's, her	90	mine

91	your	94	David's
92	yours	95	Jack and Joe's
93	David's	96	theirs

🐶 Practice 5

97　You are not Sam.
98　You are not Lucy.
99　You are not Sam and Lucy.
100　He is not David.
101　She is not Sally.
102　They are not David and Sally.
103　I am not Peter.
104　My brother is not Joe.
105　We are not Peter and Joe.
106　It is not his dog.
107　It is not his cat.
108　They are not his dog and cat.
109　This is not her key.
110　This is not her phone.
111　These are not her key and cell phone.
112　That is not their room.
113　That is not their computer.
114　Those are not their room and computer.
115　Your sister is not Kate.
116　Your brother is not Tom.
117　Your sister and brother are not Kate and Tom.

🐶 Practice 6

118　I'm not Paul.
119　I'm not your family.
120　I'm not her sister.
121　I'm not his brother.
122　I'm not their friend.
123　You're not my family.
　　　(You aren't my family.)
124　You're not her sister.
　　　(You aren't her sister.)
125　You're not his brother.
　　　(You aren't his brother.)
126　You're not our friend.
　　　(You aren't our friend.)
127　He's not my family.
　　　(He isn't my family.)
128　He's not her brother.
　　　(He isn't her brother.)
129　He's not your friend.
　　　(He isn't your friend.)
130　She's not my family.
　　　(She isn't my family.)
131　She's not his sister.
　　　(She isn't his sister.)
132　She's not their friend.
　　　(She isn't their friend.)
133　It's not my dog.
　　　(It isn't my dog.)

134 We're not family.
(We aren't family.)
135 They're not family.
(They aren't family.)
136 This isn't my dog.
137 That's not my dog.
(That isn't my dog.)
138 These aren't my pens.
139 Those aren't my bags.

🐶 Practice 7

140 Are you Lucy?
141 Are you my friend?
142 Is he David?
143 Is she Sally?
144 Are they David and Sally?
145 Are you Peter?
146 Is your brother Joe?
147 Are you Peter and Joe?
148 Is it his dog?
149 Is it his cat?
150 Are they his dog and cat?
151 Is this her key?
152 Is this her cell phone?
153 Are these her key and cell phone?
154 Is that their room?
155 Is that their computer?
156 Are those their room and computer?

157 Is your sister Kate?
158 Is your brother Tom?
159 Are your sister and brother Kate and Tom?
160 Are they your family?

🐶 Practice 8

161 Are you my friend?
Yes, I am.
No, I'm not.
162 Are you her sister?
Yes, I am.
No, I'm not.
163 Are you his brother?
Yes, I am.
No, I'm not.
164 Is he your friend?
Yes, he is.
No, he's not. = No, he isn't.
165 Is she his sister?
Yes, she is.
No, she's not. = No, she isn't.
166 Is it her dog?
Yes, it is.
No, it's not. = No, it isn't.
167 Are Billy, Judy and Sean family?
Yes, they are.
No, they aren't. = No, they're not.

168	Is it his cat?	188	You are happy.
	Yes, it is.	189	You are good.
	No, it's not. = No, it isn't.	190	You are sad.
169	Are they their pen and bag?	191	You are upset.
	Yes, they are.	192	You are tired.
	No, they aren't. = No, they're not.	193	You are bored.
170	Are they your dog and bike?	194	You are sick.
	Yes, they are.	195	You are hungry.
	No, they aren't. = No, they're not.	196	You are excited.

🐾 Practice9

171	I am happy.	201	You are tall.
172	I am good.	202	You are short.
173	I am sad.	203	You are ready.
174	I am upset.	204	You are kind(=nice).
175	I am tired.	205	He is happy.
176	I am bored.	206	He is good.
177	I am sick.	207	He is sad.
178	I am hungry.	208	He is upset.
179	I am excited.	209	He is tired.
180	I am full.	210	He is bored.
181	I am popular.	211	He is sick.
182	I am good-looking.	212	He is hungry.
183	I am smart.	213	He is excited.
184	I am tall.	214	He is full.
185	I am short.	215	He is popular.
186	I am ready.	216	He is good-looking.
187	I am kind(=nice).	217	He is smart.

(197 You are full. 198 You are popular. 199 You are good-looking. 200 You are smart.)

218	He is tall.	248	We are full.
219	He is short.	249	We are popular.
220	He is ready.	250	We are good-looking.
221	He is kind(=nice).	251	We are smart.
222	She is happy.	252	We are tall.
223	She is good.	253	We are short.
224	She is sad.	254	We are ready.
225	She is upset.	255	We are kind(=nice).
226	She is tired.	256	Sam and you are happy.
227	She is bored.	257	Sam and you are good.
228	She is sick.	258	Sam and you are sad.
229	She is hungry.	259	Sam and you are upset.
230	She is excited.	260	Sam and you are tired.
231	She is full.	261	Sam and you are bored.
232	She is popular.	262	Sam and you are sick.
233	She is good-looking.	263	Sam and you are hungry.
234	She is smart.	264	Sam and you are excited.
235	She is tall.	265	Sam and you are full.
236	She is short.	266	Sam and you are popular.
237	She is ready.	267	Sam and you are good-looking.
238	She is kind(=nice).	268	Sam and you are smart.
239	You and I are happy.	269	Sam and you are tall.
240	You and I are good.	270	Sam and you are short.
241	You and I are sad.	271	Sam and you are ready.
242	You and I are upset.	272	Sam and you are kind(=nice).
243	You and I are tired.	273	Sam and Lucy are happy.
244	You and I are bored.	274	Sam and Lucy are good.
245	You and I are sick.	275	Sam and Lucy are sad.
246	You and I are hungry.	276	Sam and Lucy are upset.
247	You and I are excited.	277	Sam and Lucy are tired.

278	Sam and Lucy are bored.
279	Sam and Lucy are sick.
280	They are hungry.
281	They are excited.
282	They are full.
283	They are popular.
284	They are good-looking.
285	They are smart.
286	They are tall.
287	They are short.
288	They are ready.
289	They are kind(=nice).
290	My dog is happy.
291	My dog is good.
292	My dog is sick.
293	My dog is smart.
294	My dog is fast.
295	My dog is quiet.
296	My dog is male.
297	His bag is blue.
298	His bag is big.
299	His bag is cute.
300	It is open.
301	It is clean.
302	It is expensive
303	It is cheap.
304	It is bad.
305	It is perfect.
306	It is slow.
307	It is yummy.
308	It is female.
309	It is white.
310	It is small.
311	It is fantastic (wonderful).
312	It is close.
313	It is dirty.
314	My sofa is comfortable.
315	My car is comfortable.
316	Their house is comfortable.
317	His plan is important.
318	Your idea is important.
319	They are important.
320	Her town is safe.
321	Ryan's house is safe.

Practice 10

322	Sam is happy.
323	Sam is a happy boy.
324	Happy Sam is my friend.
325	Lucy is pretty.
326	Lucy is a pretty girl.
327	Pretty Lucy is my sister.
328	You are special.
329	You are a special guest.
330	Mung-chi is smart.
331	Mung-chi is a smart dog.
332	Smart Mung-chi is my dog.
333	Their children are young.

334	They are young children.	377	a	
335	Their young children are cute.	378	an	
336	It is hot coffee.	379	a	
337	Hot coffee is on the table.	380	a	
338	It is her new key.	381	an	
339	Her new key is yellow.			
340	Her yellow key is heavy.			
341	This is Sam's nice laptop.			
342	Sam's nice laptop is expensive.			

Practice 11

343	a	360	a
344	a	361	a
345	an	362	a
346	a	363	an
347	a	364	an
348	an	365	a
349	a	366	an
350	a	367	a
351	an	368	a
352	an	369	an
353	a	370	a
354	a	371	a
355	an	372	an
356	a	373	a
357	a	374	an
358	an	375	a
359	a	376	a

Practice 12

382	apples
383	small apples
384	Apples
385	potatoes
386	huge potatoes
387	Potatoes
388	guests
389	special guests
390	Special guests
391	rooms
392	empty rooms
393	clean rooms
394	green benches
395	long benches
396	2 geese
397	Geese
398	feet
399	her small feet
400	Fish
401	cute fish
402	tomatoes
403	Red tomatoes
404	Red tomatoes, mine

405		candies
406		Candies
407		Sweet candies, a box
408		housewives
409		happy housewives
410		2 pianos
411		Pianos
412		People
413		quiet people
414		My parents' pictures
415		various pictures
416		my brushes
417		My brushes

431	O	부인
432	X	애플사(회사명)
433	X	돈
434	O	쿠키
435	O	선물
436	X	고기
437	X	가구

Practice 14

438	is
439	is
440	is
441	is
442	is
443	is
444	is
445	is
446	is
447	is

Practice 13

418	O	라디오
419	X	오렌지주스
420	X	로키산맥
421	X	시간
422	X	물
423	O	직업
424	O	전화기
425	X	연기
426	X	가스
427	O	동물원
428	O	달력
429	X	눈
430	O	동호회

Practice 15

448	much(a lot of, lots of)
449	some
450	little
451	not any
452	Is there any coffee in the coffee maker?
453	many(a lot of, lots of)
454	some
455	few
456	a bag of
457	2 bags of

458	not any	484	Those are the green benches.
459	Are there any snacks in your bag?	485	The benches are long.
460	much(a lot of, lots of)	486	They are the 2 geese.
461	some	487	Are the geese slow?
462	little	488	These are the shoes.
463	a glass of	489	The shoes are small and cute.
464	not any	490	The fish are in a fishbowl.
465	Is there any milk in the fridge?	491	The fish are healthy.
466	much(a lot of, lots of)	492	They are the red tomatoes.
467	some	493	The red tomatoes are really good.
468	little	494	The red tomatoes are mine.
469	2 cans of	495	They are the candies.
470	not any	496	The candies are not (aren't) sweet.
471	Is there any soda on the table?	497	The sweet candy is in a box.
		498	They are the housewives.
		499	Are the housewives happy?

🐶 Practice16

		500	These are the pianos.
		501	These pianos are expensive.
472	It is the apple.	502	The people are in the park.
473	They are the apples.	503	The people are quiet.
474	They are the sweet apples.	504	The model's photos are on the desk.
475	These are the potatoes.	505	Are those the fantastic photos?
476	They are the huge potatoes.		
477	The potato is not round.		
478	They are the guests.		
479	They are the special guests.	## 🐶 Practice17	
480	The guests are important.		
481	These are not (aren't) the rooms.	506	There are many countries on earth.
482	This is the empty room.	507	There is my(our) country on the globe.
483	The room is clean.	508	There is the country in Asia.
		509	There are many(a lot of/lots of) cities in the country.

510　There are a lot of(many, lots of) people in the city.
511　There are 3 parks in the city.
512　Is there an airport in the city?
513　Yes, there is.
514　No, there isn't.
515　There is an airport in the city.
516　There isn't an airport in the city.
517　Are there any supermarkets in the city?
518　Yes, there are.
519　No, there aren't.
520　There are many(a lot of/lots of) supermarkets in the city.
521　There aren't many(a lot of/ lots of) supermarkets in the city.
522　There isn't a supermarket in the city.
523　Is there my money on the table?
524　Yes, there is.
525　No, there's not. / No, there isn't.
526　There is much(a lot of/lots of) money on the table.
527　There is not much(a lot of/lots of) money on the table.
528　There isn't your money on the table.
529　Is there a baseball game?
530　Yes, there is.
531　No, there isn't.
532　There is a baseball game.
533　There are 2 baseball games.
534　There are not many (a lot of/ lots of) baseball games.
535　There are not any games.
536　Are there cars in the parking lot?
537　Yes, there are.
538　No, there aren't.
539　There are many cars.
540　There are not many cars.
541　There are few cars.
542　There are 2 old cars.
543　There are not any cars.

🐱 Practice 18

544　It is my cat.
545　It is my cute cat.
546　It is my cute Persian cat.
547　They are my cute cats.
548　They are my cute Persian cats.
549　This is a new movie.
550　This is an interesting new movie.
551　This is an interesting new comedy movie.
552　These are interesting new comedy movies.
553　He is an American boy.
554　He is a young American boy.
555　He is a tall American boy.
556　They are tall American boys.
557　That is a big table.
558　That is a nice big table.
559　That is a nice round table.
560　These are wooden tables.

561	Those are wooden tables.
562	Those are nice big round tables.
563	It is my new car.
564	It is my nice new car.
565	That is their new car.
566	Those are our nice new cars.
567	It is a red Italian convertible car.
568	They are red Italian convertible cars.
569	It is a small bag.
570	They are 2 small bags.
571	They are 2 small yellow bags.
572	It is a black plastic bag.
573	They are 2 black plastic bags.

Practice 19

574	Sam is really happy.
575	Sam is really really happy.
576	I am very hungry. 나는 정말 배고파.
577	Actually, she is my friend. 사실, 걔 내 친구야.
578	We are full very much. 우리는 배가 많이 불러.
579	Fortunately, my mom is in the house. 다행히, 엄마는 집에 계셔.

Practice 20

580	Buses are very fast.
581	The subway is very safe.
582	This is really important information.

Practice 21

583	X (필요하지 않음)	587	sometimes
584	always	588	never
585	hardly	589	usually
586	often	590	not

Practice 22

591	knows	604	finds
592	borrows	605	understands
593	draws	606	brings
594	rains	607	cancels
595	listens	608	travels
596	explains	609	sells
597	becomes	610	counts
598	agrees	611	waits
599	saves	612	forgets
600	leaves	613	starts
601	believes	614	breaks
602	hides	615	displays
603	needs	616	supplies

617 finishes
618 launches
619 focuses
620 practices

🐾 Practice23

621 I like Sam.
622 You like Sam.
623 His father likes Sam.
624 He likes Sam.
625 His mother likes Sam.
626 She likes Sam.
627 His dog likes Sam.
628 My sister likes Sam.
629 Sunny and I like Sam.
630 We like Sam.
631 Sunny and the girl like Sam.
632 They like Sam.
633 I have a dog.
634 You have a dog.
635 Sam has a dog.
636 He has a dog.
637 Lucy has a dog.
638 She has a dog.
639 Lucy and I have dogs.
640 We have dogs.
641 Jacob and you have dogs.
642 You have dogs.
643 Grace and Sam have dogs.
644 They have dogs.
645 I go to school.
646 You go to school.
647 Amy goes to school.
648 She goes to school.
649 Sam goes to school.
650 He goes to school.
651 My dog goes to school.
652 My brother goes to school.
653 Lucy and I go to school.
654 We go to school.
655 Sarah and you go home.
656 You go home.
657 Sarah and Emily go home.
658 They go home.
659 I study.
660 You study.
661 Kevin studies.
662 He studies.
663 Lucy studies.
664 She studies.
665 Kevin and I study.
666 We study.
667 Ethan and you study.
668 You study.
669 Jacob and Kevin study.
670 They study.
671 I drink a cup of milk in the morning.
672 You drink a cup of milk in the morning.
673 He drinks a cup of milk in the morning.
674 She drinks a cup of milk in the morning.

675	Sam and I drink a cup of milk in the morning.			704	herself	720	themselves

675 Sam and I drink a cup of milk in the morning.
676 Jenny and you drink a cup of milk in the morning.
677 We drink a cup of milk in the morning.
678 I do exercise in the park every day.
679 You do exercise in the park every day.
680 We do exercise in the park every day.
681 The handsome boy does exercise in the park every day.
682 She does exercise in the park every day.
683 Emma does exercise in the park every day.
684 Emma and the boy do exercise in the park every day.
685 They do exercise in the park every day.

704 herself
705 them
706 children
707 ourselves
708 me
709 you
710 her
711 their parents
712 themselves
713 myself
714 him
715 yourself
716 your brother
717 himself
718 Lucy
719 herself

720 themselves
721 ourselves
722 myself
723 yourself
724 himself
725 herself
726 ourselves
727 themselves
728 myself
729 yourself
730 himself
731 herself
732 themselves
733 yourselves
734 ourselves
735 themselves

Practice 24

686 you
687 him
688 her
689 them
690 myself
691 me
692 yourself
693 him
694 her
695 us
696 them
697 me
698 himself
699 you
700 her
701 me
702 us
703 yourselves

Practice 25

736 You make me happy.
737 You make me sad.
738 You make me cheerful.
739 You make me upset.
740 You make me annoyed.
741 Sam makes her happy.
742 Sam makes her sad.
743 Sam makes her cheerful.
744 Sam makes her upset.
745 Sam makes her annoyed.

746　Lucy makes them happy.
747　Lucy makes them sad.
748　Lucy makes them cheerful.
749　Lucy makes them upset.
750　Lucy makes them annoyed.
751　Beautiful flowers make people happy.
752　Terrible news makes people sad.
753　Strong belief makes people cheerful.
754　Impolite behavior makes people upset.
755　Humid and hot weather makes people annoyed.

 Practice26

756　I do not(=don't) like Sam.
　　Do I like Sam?
　　Yes, you do.
　　No, you don't(=do not).
757　You do not(=don't) like Sam.
　　Do you like Sam?
　　Yes, I do. / Yes, we do.
　　No, I don't(=do not). / No, we don't.
758　His father does not(doesn't) like Sam.
　　Does his father like Sam?
　　Yes, he does.
　　No, he doesn't(=does not).
759　He does not(doesn't) like Sam.
　　Does he like Sam?
　　Yes, he does.
　　No, he doesn't(=does not).
760　His mother does not(doesn't) like Sam.
　　Does his mother like Sam?
　　Yes, she does.
　　No, she doesn't(=does not).
761　She does not(doesn't) like Sam.
　　Does she like Sam?
　　Yes, she does.
　　No, she doesn't(=does not).
762　His dog does not(doesn't) like Sam.
　　Does his dog like Sam?
　　Yes, it does.
　　No, it doesn't(=does not).
763　It does not(doesn't) like Sam.
　　Does it like Sam?
　　Yes, it does.
　　No, it doesn't(=does not).
764　Sunny and I do not(=don't) like Sam.
　　Do Sunny and I like Sam?
　　Yes, you do.
　　No, you don't(=do not).
765　We do not(=don't) like Sam.
　　Do we like Sam?
　　Yes, you do.
　　No, you don't(=do not).
766　Sunny and the girl do not(=don't) like Sam.

Do Sunny and the girl like Sam?

Yes, they do.

No, they don't(=do not).

767 They do not(=don't) like Sam.

Do they like Sam?

Yes, they do.

No, they don't(=do not).

768 I do not(=don't) have a dog.

Do I have a dog?

Yes, you do.

No, you don't(=do not).

769 You do not(=don't) have a dog.

Do you have a dog?

Yes, I do. / Yes, we do.

No, I don't(=do not). / No, we don't.

770 Sam does not(=doesn't) have a dog.

Does Sam have a dog?

Yes, he does.

No, he doesn't(=does not).

771 He does not(=doesn't) have a dog.

Does he have a dog?

Yes, he does.

No, he doesn't(=does not).

772 Lucy does not(=doesn't) have a dog.

Does Lucy have a dog?

Yes, she does.

No, she doesn't(=does not).

773 She does not(=doesn't) have a dog.

Does she have a dog?

Yes, she does.

No, she doesn't(=does not).

774 Lucy and I do not(=don't) have dogs.

Do Lucy and I have dogs?

Yes, you do.

No, you don't(=do not).

775 We do not(=don't) have dogs.

Do we have dogs?

Yes, you do.

No, you don't(=do not).

776 Sunny and you do not(=don't) have dogs.

Do Sunny and you have dogs?

Yes, we do.

No, we don't(=do not).

777 You do not(=don't) have dogs.

Do you have dogs?

Yes, I do. / Yes, we do.

No, I don't(=do not). / No, we don't.

778 Lucy and Sam do not(=don't) have dogs.

Do Lucy and Sam have dogs?

Yes, they do.

No, they don't(=do not).

779 They do not(=don't) have dogs.

Do they have dogs?

Yes, they do.

No, they don't(=do not).

780 I do not(=don't) go to school.

Do I go to school?

Yes, you do.

No, you don't(=do not).

781 You do not(=don't) go to school.
Do you go to school?
Yes, I do. / Yes, we do.
No, I don't(=do not). / No, we don't.

782 Sunny does not(=doesn't) go to school.
Does Sunny go to school?
Yes, she does.
No, she doesn't(=does not).

783 She does not(=doesn't) go to school.
Does she go to school?
Yes, she does.
No, she doesn't(=does not).

784 Sam does not(=doesn't) go to school.
Does Sam go to school?
Yes, he does.
No, he doesn't(=does not).

785 He does not(=doesn't) go to school.
Does he go to school?
Yes, he does.
No, he doesn't(=does not).

786 My dog does not(=doesn't) go to school.
Does my dog go to school?
Yes, it does.
No, it doesn't(=does not).

787 It does not(=doesn't) go to school.
Does it go to school?
Yes, it does.
No, it doesn't(=does not).

788 Lucy and I do not(=don't) go to school.
Do Lucy and I go to school?
Yes, you do.
No, you don't(=do not).

789 We do not(=don't) go to school.
Do we go to school?
Yes, you do.
No, you don't(do not).

790 Sunny and you do not(=don't) go home.
Do Sunny and you go home?
Yes, we do.
No, we don't(=do not).

791 You do not(=don't) go home.
Do you go home?
Yes, I do. / Yes, we do.
No, I don't(=do not). / No, we don't.

792 Sunny and Lucy do not(=don't) go home.
Do Sunny and Lucy go home?
Yes, they do.
No, they don't(=do not).

793 They do not(=don't) go home.
Do they go home?
Yes, they do.
No, they don't(=do not).

794 I do not(=don't) study.
Do I study?
Yes, you do.
No, you don't(=do not).

795 You do not(=don't) study.
Do you study?

Yes, I do. / Yes, we do.

No, I don't(=do not). / No, we don't.

796 Sam does not(=doesn't) study.

Does Sam study?

Yes, he does.

No, he doesn't(does not).

797 He does not(=doesn't) study.

Does he study?

Yes, he does.

No, he doesn't(=does not).

798 Lucy does not(=doesn't) study.

Does she study?

Yes, she does.

No, she doesn't(=does not).

799 She does not(=doesn't) study.

Does she study?

Yes, she does.

No, she doesn't(=does not).

800 Sam and I do not(=don't) study.

Do Sam and I study?

Yes, you do.

No, you don't(=do not).

801 We do not(=don't) study.

Do we study?

Yes, you do.

No, you don't(=do not).

802 Sunny and you do not(=don't) study.

Do Sunny and you study?

Yes, we do.

No, we don't(=do not).

803 The children do not(=don't) study.

Do the children study?

Yes, they do.

No, they don't(=do not).

804 Lucy and Sunny do not(=don't) study.

Do Lucy and Sunny study?

Yes, they do.

No, they don't(=do not).

805 They do not(=don't) study.

Do they study?

Yes, they do.

No, they don't(=do not).

806 I do not(=don't) drink a cup of milk

in the morning.

Do I drink a cup of milk in the morning?

Yes, you do.

No, you don't(=do not).

807 You do not(=don't) drink a cup of

milk in the morning.

Do you drink a cup of milk

in the morning?

Yes, I do. / Yes, we do.

No, I don't(=do not). / No, we don't.

808 He does not(=doesn't) drink a cup of

milk in the morning.

Does he drink a cup of milk

in the morning?

Yes, he does.

No, he doesn't(=does not).

809 She does not(=doesn't) drink a cup

of milk in the morning.

Does she drink a cup of milk in the morning?
Yes, she does.
No, she doesn't(=does not).

810 Sam and I do not(=don't) drink a cup of milk in the morning.
Do Sam and I drink a cup of milk in the morning?
Yes, you do.
No, you don't(=do not).

811 Sunny and you do not(=don't) drink a cup of milk in the morning.
Do Sunny and you drink a cup of milk in the morning?
Yes, we do.
No, we don't(=do not).

812 We do not(=don't) drink a cup of milk in the morning.
Do we drink a cup of milk in the morning?
Yes, you do.
No, you don't(=do not).

813 I do not(=don't) take a walk in the park every day.
Do I take a walk in the park every day?
Yes, you do. /No, you don't(=do not).

814 You do not(=don't) take a walk in the park every day.
Do you take a walk in the park every day?
Yes, I do. / Yes, we do.
No, I don't(=do not). / No, we don't.

815 My sister does not(=doesn't) take a walk in the park every day.
Does my sister take a walk in the park every day?
Yes, she does.
No, she doesn't(=does not).

816 We do not(=don't) take a walk in the park every day.
Do we take a walk in the park every day?
Yes, you do.
No, you don't(=do not).

817 The handsome boy does not(=doesn't) take a walk in the park every day.
Does the handsome boy take a walk in the park every day?
Yes, he does.
No, he doesn't(=does not).

818 Lucy does not(=doesn't) take a walk in the park every day.
Does Lucy take a walk in the park every day?
Yes, she does.
No, she doesn't(=does not).

819 Lucy and the boy do not (=don't) take a walk in the park every day.
Do Lucy and the boy take a walk in the park every day?
Yes, they do.
No, they don't(=do not).

820 They do not(=don't) take a walk in the park every day.
Do they take a walk in the park every day?
Yes, they do.
No, they don't(=do not).

Practice 27

821	was	나는 행복했어.
822	was	샘은 행복했어.
823	were	우리는 행복했어.
824	was	샘은 학생이었어.
825	was	나는 학생이었어.
826	were	샘과 나는 학생이었어.
827	was	데이빗은 친절한 소년이었어.
828	was	샘은 친절한 소년이었어
829	were	그들은 친절한 소년이었어.
830	was	샘은 나랑 매우 친했어.
831	were	너는 샘이랑 매우 친했어.
832	were	샘과 너는 매우 친했어.
833	was	나는 작년에 중국에 있었어.
834	was	그녀는 작년에 중국에 있었어.
835	were	우리는 작년에 중국에 있었어.
836	was	그는 어제 아팠어.
837	were	너는 어제 아팠어.
838	were	샘과 너는 어제 아팠어.

Practice 28

839 The ring was very expensive.
840 The price was reasonable.
841 Her adorable baby was 2 years old last year.
842 Her popular younger brother was 21 years old last year.
843 I was at home with my friend.
844 My friend and I were at home.
845 The short chubby boy was next to me.
846 10 travelers were next to me.
847 A beautiful woman is next to me now.
848 There was much (a lot of/lots of) juice on the table.
849 The pizza was really good and the salad was fresh.
850 We were full.

Practice 29

851	d	860	t
852	d	861	d
853	d	862	d
854	d	863	t
855	d	864	t
856	d	865	t
857	d	866	t
858	d	867	t
859	d	868	t

869	t	875	Id
870	t	876	Id
871	Id	877	Id
872	Id	878	Id
873	Id	879	Id
874	Id	880	Id

Practice30

881	liked	901	had
882	liked	902	had
883	liked	903	had
884	likes	904	had
885	liked	905	went
886	likes	906	went
887	liked	907	went
888	likes	908	went
889	liked	909	went
890	liked	910	went
891	liked	911	went
892	liked	912	go
893	has	913	went
894	have	914	went
895	have	915	studied
896	had	916	studied
897	had	917	studied
898	had	918	studied
899	had	919	studied
900	had	920	studies

Practice31

921 She took an airplane last year.
922 She traveled Europe.
923 She took many beautiful pictures.
924 We did our homework.
925 We had many questions.
926 We asked them to our teacher.
927 My sister cleaned her room.
928 She washed the dishes in the kitchen.
 / She did the dishes in the kitchen.
929 She exercised with me in the gym.
930 She and I had dinner at a family restaurant.

Practice32

931 나는 샘을 좋아했어.
 I did not(didn't) like Sam.
932 샘은 친절했어.
 Sam was not(wasn't) kind.
933 너는 샘을 좋아했어.
 You did not(didn't) like Sam.
934 데이빗은 샘을 좋아했어.
 David did not(didn't) like Sam.
935 애완동물(들)은 샘을 좋아했어.
 Pets did not(didn't) like Sam.
936 바구니에 더러운 옷들이 있었어.
 There were not(weren't) dirty clothes in the basket.

937 그것들은 냄새났어.
They were not(weren't) stinky.

938 나는 빨래했어.
I did not(didn't) do the laundry.

939 우리 엄마가 다시 빨래를 하셨어.
My mother did not(didn't) do the laundry again.

940 내 남동생과 여동생이 오늘 아침 빨래를 했어.
My brother and sister did not(didn't) do the laundry this morning.

941 개들이 애완동물 가게에 있었어.
Dogs were not(weren't) in the pet shop.

942 나는 개를 키웠어.
I did not(didn't) have a dog.

943 너(희)는 개를 키웠어.
You did not(didn't) have a dog.

944 루시는 개를 키웠어.
Lucy did not(didn't) have a dog.

945 우리는 개를 키웠어.
We did not(didn't) have a dog.

946 나는 집에 있었어.
I was not(wasn't) at home.

947 우리 오빠는 학교에 갔어.
My brother did not(didn't) go to school.

948 샘은 학교에 갔어.
Sam did not(didn't) go to school.

949 내 친구들은 학교에 갔어.
My friends did not(didn't) go to school.

950 그들은 학교에 갔어.
They did not(didn't) go to school.

951 중간고사에 많은 과목이 있었어.
There were not(weren't) a lot of subjects for the midterm exam.

952 나는 수학을 공부했어.
I did not(didn't) study math.

953 에이미는 과학을 공부했어.
Amy did not(didn't) study science.

954 라이언은 역사를 공부했어.
Ryan did not(didn't) study history.

955 마이클은 영어를 공부했어.
Michael did not(didn't) study English.

956 그녀는 곤경에 빠졌었어.
She was not(wasn't) in trouble.

957 그녀는 나의 도움을 필요로 했어.
She did not(didn't) need my help.

958 그녀는 (그녀의) 선생님의 도움을 필요로 했어.
She did not(didn't) need her teacher's help.

959 그녀는 그들의 도움을 필요로 했어.
She did not(didn't) need their help.

960 샘은 너의 도움을 필요로 했어.
She did not(didn't) need your help.

961 지난여름은 너무 더웠어.
It was not(wasn't) so hot last summer.

962 지난여름에 그 해변은 너무 붐볐어.
The beach was not(wasn't) very crowded last summer.

963 많은 사람이 붐비는 곳(들)을 싫어했어.
Many people did not(didn't) hate crowded places.

964 많은 사람들이 그 도시를 싫어했어.
Many people did not(didn't) hate the city.

965 많은 아이들이 길거리 음식을 싫어했어.
Many children did not(didn't) hate street food.

966 책장에 많은책이 있었어.
There were not(weren't) many books in the bookcase.

967 피터는 만화책을 읽었어.
Peter did not(didn't) read a comic book.

968 그의 아버지는 소설을 읽으셨어.
His father did not(didn't) read a novel.

969 그의 어머니는 자동차 잡지를 읽으셨어.
His mother did not(didn't) read a car magazine.

970 그들은 요리책을 읽었어.
They did not(didn't) read a cookbook.

971 테이블에 많은 쿠키가 있었어.
There were not(weren't) a lot of cookies on the table.

972 나는 쿠키를 우유랑 같이 먹었어.
I did not(didn't) have cookies with milk.

973 엄마는 나에게 쿠키를 만들어 주셨어.
My mother did not(didn't) make me cookies.

974 쿠키는 정말 맛있었어.
The cookies did not(didn't) taste great.

975 나는 내 동생(여)에게 쿠키를 주었어.
I did not(didn't) give my sister cookies.

Practice33

976 Did I like Sam?
Yes, you did.
No, you didn't.

977 Was Sam kind?
Yes, he was.
No, he wasn't.

978 Did you like Sam?
Yes, I did. / Yes, we did.
No, I didn't. / No, we didn't.

979 Did David like Sam?
Yes, he did.
No, he didn't.

980 Did pets like Sam?
Yes, they did.
No, they didn't.

981 Were there many dirty clothes in the basket?
Yes, there were.
No, there weren't.

982 Were they stinky?

Yes, they were.

No, they weren't.

983 Did I do the laundry?

Yes, you did.

No, you didn't.

984 Did my mother do the laundry again?

Yes, she did.

No, she didn't.

985 Did my brother and sister do the laundry this morning?

Yes, they did.

No, they didn't.

986 Were dogs in the pet shop?

Yes, they were.

No, they weren't.

987 Did I have a dog?

Yes, you did.

No, you didn't.

988 Did you have a dog?

Yes, I did. / Yes, we did.

No, I didn't. / No, we didn't.

989 Did Lucy have a dog?

Yes, she did.

No, she didn't.

990 Did we have a dog?

Yes, you did.

No, you didn't.

991 Was I at home?

Yes, you were.

No, you weren't.

992 Did my brother go to school?

Yes, he did.

No, he didn't.

993 Did Sam go to school?

Yes, he did.

No, he didn't.

994 Did my friends go to school?

Yes, they did.

No, they didn't.

995 Did they go to school?

Yes, they did.

No, they didn't.

996 Were there a lot of subjects for the midterm exam?

Yes, there were.

No, there weren't.

997 Did I study math?

Yes, you did.

No, you didn't.

998 Did Amy study science?

Yes, she did.

No, she didn't.

999 Did Ryan study history?

Yes, he did.

No, he didn't.

1000 Did Michael study English?

Yes, he did.

No, he didn't.

1001 Was she in trouble?

Yes, she was.

No, she wasn't.

1002 Did she need my help?
Yes, she did.
No, she didn't.

1003 Did she need her teacher's help?
Yes, she did.
No, she didn't.

1004 Did she need their help?
Yes, she did.
No, she didn't.

1005 Did she need your help?
Yes, she did.
No, she didn't.

1006 Was it so hot last summer?
Yes, it was.
No, it wasn't.

1007 Was the beach very crowded last summer?
Yes, it was.
No, it wasn't.

1008 Did many people hate crowded places?
Yes, they did.
No, they didn't.

1009 Did many people hate the city?
Yes, they did.
No, they didn't.

1010 Did many children hate street food?
Yes, they did.
No, they didn't.

1011 Were there many books in the bookcase?
Yes, there were. / No, there weren't.

1012 Did Peter read a dictionary?
Yes, he did.
No, he didn't.

1013 Did his father read a novel?
Yes, he did.
No, he didn't.

1014 Did his mother read a car magazine?
Yes, she did.
No, she didn't.

1015 Did they read a cookbook?
Yes, they did.
No, they didn't.

1016 Were there a lot of cookies on the table?
Yes, there were.
No, there weren't.

1017 Did I have cookies with milk?
Yes, you did.
No, you didn't.

1018 Did my mother make me cookies?
Yes, she did.
No, she didn't.

1019 Did the cookies taste great?
Yes, they did.
No, they didn't.

1020 Did I give my sister cookies?

Yes, you did.

No, you didn't.

Practice34

조니는 작년에 15세였어. 조니는 작년에 캐나다에 살았는데, 지금은 한국에 살아. 조니는 지난주 토요일에 집에 있었어. 조니는 TV에서 하는 코미디 쇼를 좋아했어.

1021 조니는 지난주 토요일에 학교에 갔어?
No, he didn't.

1022 조니는 지금 캐나다에 살아?
No, he doesn't.

1023 조니는 작년에 14살이었어?
No, he wasn't.

1024 조니는 코미디 쇼를 좋아했어?
Yes, he did.

1025 조니는 작년에 한국에 있었어?
No, he wasn't.

 Practice35

1026 (문제) 나는 걸어.
I am walking.

1027 (문제) 그 어린 소녀가 걸어.
The young girl is walking.

1028 (문제) 너는 걸어.
You are walking.

1029 (문제) 준과 그녀는 걸어.
June and she are walking.

1030 (문제) 그들은 걸어.
They are walking.

1031 (문제) 나는 과자를 좀 먹어.
I am eating some snacks.

1032 (문제) 걔는 과자를 좀 먹어.
She is eating some snacks.

1033 (문제) 너(희)는 과자를 좀 먹어.
You are eating some snacks.

1034 (문제) 샐리와 걔는 과자를 좀 먹어.
Sally and he are eating some snacks.

1035 (문제) 우리는 과자를 좀 먹어.
We are eating some snacks.

1036 (문제) 나는 달렸어.
I was running.

1037 (문제) 너는 달렸어.
You were running.

1038 (문제) 내 친구, 닉은 달렸어.
My friend, Nick was running.

1039 (문제) 너와 나는 달렸어.
You and I were running.

1040 (문제) 우리는 달렸어.
We were running.

1041 (문제) 나는 백화점에 가.
I am going to the department store.

1042 (문제) 너는 백화점에 가.
You are going to the department store.

1043 (문제) 그는 백화점에 가.
He is going to the department store.

1044 (문제) 너와 나는 백화점에 가.
You and I are going to the department store.

1045 (문제) 피터와 루시는 백화점에 가.
Peter and Lucy are going to the department store.

1046 (문제) 걔네들은 백화점에 가.
They are going to the department store.

1047 (문제) 나는 책을 읽어(읽었어).
I am(was) reading a book.

1048 (문제) 내 친구는 책을 읽어.
My friend is reading a book.

1049 (문제) 우리는 책을 읽어(읽었어).
We are(were) reading a book.

1050 (문제) 그녀의 선생님은 책을 읽으셔.
Her teacher is reading a book.

1051 (문제) 나의 똑똑하고 잘생긴 삼촌은 책을 읽으셔.
My smart handsome uncle is reading a book.

1052 (문제) 그들은 책을 읽어(읽었어).
They are(were) reading a book.

1053 (문제) 나는 일했어.
I was working.

1054 (문제) 너는 일했어.
You were working.

1055 (문제) 우리 아빠는 일하셨어.
My father was working.

1056 (문제) 그의 누나는 일했어.
His sister was working.

1057 (문제) 많은 사람들이 일했어.
A lot of people were working.

1058 (문제) 그들은 일했어.
They were working.

1059 (문제) 나는 내 차를 운전해.
I am driving my car.

1060 (문제) 너(희)는 너의(희) 형 차를 운전해.
You are driving your brother's car.

1061 (문제) 그는 자기 누나의 차를 운전해.
He is driving his sister's car.

1062 (문제) 그녀는 자기 아버지의 차를 운전해.
She is driving her father's car.

1063 (문제) 나의 엄마와 할머니는 그 차(들)를 운전해.
My mother and grandmother are driving the cars.

1064 (문제) 그들은 그의 차를 운전해.
They are driving his car.

1065 (문제) 나는 영어를 (말)했어.
I was speaking English.

1066 (문제) 너는 영어를 (말)했어.
You were speaking English.

1067 (문제) 우리는 영어를 (말)했어.
We were speaking English.

1068 (문제) 걔(남자)는 영어를 (말)했어.
He was speaking English.

1069 (문제) 걔(여자)는 영어를 (말)했어.
She was speaking English.

1070 (문제) 그들은 영어를 (말)했어.
They were speaking English.

Practice 36

1071 Am I walking?
Yes, you are.
No, you aren't. / No, you're not.

1072 Is the slim girl walking?
Yes, she is.
No, she isn't. / No, she's not.

1073 Are you walking?
Yes, I am. / Yes, we are.
No, I'm not. / No, we're not (aren't).

1074 Are June and she walking?
Yes, they are.
No, they aren't. / No, they're not.

1075 Are they walking?
Yes, they are.
No, they aren't. / No, they're not.

1076 Am I eating any snacks?
Yes, you are.
No, you aren't. / No, you're not.

1077 Is she eating any snacks?
Yes, she is.
No, she isn't. / No, she's not.

1078 Are you eating any snacks?
Yes, I am. / Yes, we are.
No, I'm not. / No, we're not (aren't).

1079 Are Sally and he eating any snacks?
Yes, they are.
No, they aren't. / No, they're not.

1080 Are we eating any snacks?
Yes, you are.
No, you aren't. / No, you're not.

1081 Was I running?
Yes, you were.
No, you weren't.

1082 Were you running?
Yes, I was. / Yes, we were.
No, I wasn't. / No, we weren't.

1083 Was my friend, Nick running?
Yes, he was.
No, he wasn't.

1084 Were you and I running?
Yes, we were.
No, we weren't.

1085 Were we running?
Yes, you were.
No, you weren't.

1086 Am I going to the department store?
Yes, you are.
No, you aren't. / No, you're not.

1087 Are you going to the department store?
Yes, I am. / Yes, we are.
No, I'm not. / No, we're not (aren't).

1088 Is he going to the department store?
Yes, he is.
No, he's not. / No, he isn't.

1089 Are you and I going to the department store?
Yes, we are.
No, we aren't / No, we're not.

1090 Are Peter and Lucy going to the department store?
Yes, they are.
No, they aren't. / No, they're not.

1091 Are they going to the department store?
Yes, they are.
No, they aren't. / No, they're not.

1092 Am I reading a book?
Yes, you are.
No, you aren't. / No, you're not.

1093 Is my friend reading a book?
Yes, he(she) is.
No, he(she) isn't.
/ No, he's(she's) not.

1094 Are we reading a book?
Yes, you are.
No, you aren't.

1095 Is her teacher reading a book?
Yes, he(she) is.
No, he(she) isn't.

1096 Is my smart handsome uncle reading a book?
Yes, he is.
No, he isn't. / No, he's not.

1097 Are they reading a book?
Yes, they are.
No, they aren't. / No, they're not.

1098 Was I working?
Yes, you were.
No, you weren't.

1099 Were you working?
Yes, I was. / Yes, we were.
No, I wasn't. / No, we weren't.

1100 Was my father working?
Yes, he was.
No, he wasn't.

1101 Was his sister working?
Yes, she was.
No, she wasn't.

1102 Were a lot of people working?
Yes, they were.
No, they weren't.

1103 Were they working?
Yes, they were.
No, they weren't.

1104 Am I driving my car?
Yes, you are.
No, you aren't. / No, you're not.

1105 Are you driving your car?
Yes, I am. / Yes, we are.
No, I'm not. / No, we aren't.

1106 Is he driving his sister's car?
Yes, he is.
No, he isn't. / No, he's not.

1107 Is she driving her father's car?
Yes, she is.
No, she isn't. / No, she's not.

1108 Are my mother and grandmother driving the cars?
Yes, they are.
No, they aren't. / No, they're not.

1109 Are they driving his car?
Yes, they are.
No, they aren't. / No, they're not.

1110 Was I speaking English?
Yes, you were.
No, you weren't.

1111 Were you speaking English?
Yes, I was. / Yes, we were.
No, I wasn't. / No, we weren't.

1112 Were we speaking English?
Yes, you were.
No, you weren't.

1113 Was he speaking English?
Yes, he was.
No, he wasn't.

1114 Was she speaking English?
Yes, she was.
No, she wasn't.

1115 Were they speaking English?
Yes, they were.
No, they weren't.

Practice 37

1116 I am(I'm) not walking.
1117 The slim girl is not(isn't) walking.
1118 You are not(aren't) walking.
1119 June and she are not(aren't) walking.
1120 They are not(aren't) walking.
1121 I am(I'm) not eating any snacks.
1122 She is not(isn't) eating any snacks.
1123 You are not(aren't) eating any snacks.
1124 Sally and he are not(aren't) eating any snacks.
1125 We are not(aren't) eating any snacks.
1126 I was not(wasn't) running.
1127 You were not(weren't) running.
1128 My friend, Nick was not(wasn't) running.
1129 You and I were not(weren't) running.
1130 We were not(weren't) running.
1131 I am(I'm) not going to the department store.
1132 You are not(aren't) going to the department store.
1133 He is not(isn't) going to the department store.
1134 You and I are not(aren't) going to the department store.
1135 Peter and Lucy are not(aren't) going to the department store.
1136 They are not(aren't) going to the department store.
1137 I am(I'm) not reading a book.
1138 My friend is not(isn't) reading a book.
1139 We are not(aren't) reading a book.
1140 Her teacher is not(isn't) reading a book.
1141 My smart handsome uncle is not (isn't) reading a book.

1142 They are not(aren't) reading a book.
1143 I was not(wasn't) working.
1144 You were not(weren't) working.
1145 My father was not(wasn't) working.
1146 His sister was not(wasn't) working.
1147 A lot of people were not(weren't) working.
1148 They were not(weren't) working.
1149 I am(I'm) not driving my car.
1150 You are not(aren't) driving your car.
1151 He is not(isn't) driving his sister's car.
1152 She is not(isn't) driving her father's car.
1153 My mother and grandmother are not(aren't) driving the cars.
1154 They are not(aren't) driving his car.
1155 I was not(wasn't) speaking English.
1156 You were not(weren't) speaking English.
1157 We were not(weren't) speaking English.
1158 He was not(wasn't) speaking English.
1159 She was not(wasn't) speaking English.
1160 They were not(weren't) speaking English.

Practice 38

1161 Sam and I must go there.
1162 You should go there.
1163 I will go there.
1164 Jenny may go there.
1165 Lucy can go there.
1166 My sister could go there.
1167 You may go there.
1168 You must be at the cafe.
1169 You should be at the cafe.
1170 I will be at the cafe.
1171 Sam may(might) be at the cafe.
1172 Peter will attend the meeting.
1173 Peter would attend the meeting.
1174 I can attend the meeting.
1175 Lucy could attend the meeting.
1176 You should attend the meeting.
1177 Sam must attend the meeting.
1178 He may(might) attend the meeting.

Practice 39

1179 We must not smoke in the hospital.
1180 He should not(shouldn't) be alone in the house.
1181 They will not(won't) come to her birthday party.
1182 I will not(won't) make my friends sad.

1183 She would not(may not) call him.

1184 I can't go to the concert with you.

1185 We can't agree with it.

1186 He could not(couldn't) cheat on the test.

1187 They could not(couldn't) buy the bags yesterday.

1188 It may(might) not be true.

1189 You should not(shouldn't) exercise.

Practice40

1190 그는 집에 혼자 있는 게 좋아.
Should he be alone in the house?

1191 그들은 그녀의 생일파티에 올 거야.
Will they come to her birthday party?

1192 좋은 점수는 나를 행복하게 해.
Will a good score make me happy?

1193 넌 나랑 그 콘서트에 갈 수 있어.
Can you go to the concert with me?

1194 너는 그것에 동의할 수 있어.
Can you agree with it?

1195 그는 그 시험에서 컨닝할 수 있어.(아닐 수도 있고.)
Could he cheat on the test?

1196 걔(여자)가 나한테 전화할 거야.
Will she call me?

1197 그는 금메달을 딸 수 있어.(아닐 수도 있고)
Could he win a gold medal?

1198 그들은 어제 그 가방(들)을 살 수 있었어.
Could they buy the bags yesterday?

1199 너는 네 방에서 쉬어도 돼.
May I rest in your room?

1200 루시는 아마 열쇠를 가지고 있을 거야.
May Lucy have a key?

Practice41

1201 그를 위해 선물을 사는 게 좋을까?
Yes, you/we should.

1202 토요일에 일하는 게 좋을까?
No, you shouldn't.

1203 지금 자러 갈 거야?
Yes, I will.

1204 샘과 팀이 다음주에 너를 만나러 올까?
Yes, they will.

1205 내일 걔(여자)가 그 컴퓨터 사용할 거야?
Well, she would.

1206 너의 전화 번호를 내게 말해줄 수 있어?
Sure. / Of course.

1207 그 선생님은 내 질문들에 답할 수 있을까?
Yes, she(he) can.

1208 너(희)는 기타를 칠(연주할) 수 있어?
Yes, I can. / Yes, we can.

1209 그 자를 건네 줄래(주시겠어요)?
Sure. / Of course.

1210 이 자리에 앉아도 될까요?
No, you may not.

Practice42

1211 I played very interesting computer games yesterday.
1212 I visited them late.
1213 I opened the door quietly, too.
1214 My mom still waited for me in the living room.
1215 She looked very upset.
1216 I told her quickly.
1217 Suddenly, she shouted loudly.
1218 I said the reason again and again.
1219 She doesn't sometimes listen to me carefully.
1220 My father came back home with very delicious fried chicken.
1221 Fried chicken is always our favorite.
1222 My mom always acts wisely.
1223 She forgave me generously.
1224 We sat at the table and ate it happily.
1225 I love my family so much.

Practice43

1226 Isn't he Sam?
　　 Yes, he is.
　　 No, he isn't. / No, he's not.
1227 Aren't you Sam?
　　 Yes, I am.
　　 No, I'm not.
1228 Aren't they Lucy and David?
　　 Yes, they are.
　　 No, they aren't. / No, they're not.
1229 Aren't you happy?
　　 Yes, we are.
　　 No, we're not. / No, we aren't.
1230 Aren't you hungry?
　　 Yes, I am.
　　 No, I'm not.
1231 Wasn't he your teacher?
　　 Yes, he was.
　　 No, he wasn't.
1232 Weren't they your friends?
　　 Yes, they were.
　　 No, they weren't.
1233 Weren't your new clothes clean?
　　 Yes, they were.
　　 No, they weren't.
1234 Don't you know Sam?
　　 Yes, I do.
　　 No, I don't.
1235 Doesn't Sam study hard?
　　 Yes, he does.
　　 No, he doesn't.
1236 Didn't she lose her key?
　　 Yes, she did.
　　 No, she didn't.

1237 Didn't your father and mother take a trip?
Yes, they did.
No, they didn't.

1238 Can't you speak Spanish?
Yes, I can.
No, I can't.

1239 Can't you drive?
Yes, I can.
No, I can't.

1240 Didn't the man take my photos?
Yes, he did.
No, he didn't.

Practice44

1241 걔는 샘이지, 그렇지 않아?
No, he isn't. / No, he's not.

1242 샘은 행복해, 그렇지 않아?
Yes, he is.

1243 샘은 화나지 않았어, 그렇지?
Yes, he is.

1244 샘은 똑똑하고 관대해, 그렇지 않아?
No, he isn't. / No, he's not.

1245 샘은 열심히 공부해, 그렇지 않아?
Yes, he does.

1246 샘은 벌레(들)를 좋아하지 않아, 그렇지?
No, he doesn't.

1247 샘은 지난 겨울 스키를 타러 가지 않았어, 그렇지?
Yes, he did.

1248 샘은 가끔 체육관에 갔어, 그렇지 않아?
No, he didn't.

1249 샘은 농구를 매우 잘 할 수 있어, 그렇지 않아?
Yes, he can.

1250 샘은 춤을 잘 출 수 없어, 그렇지?
No, he can't.

1251 너(희)는 피곤해, 그렇지 않아?
No, I'm not. / No, we aren't.

1252 너(희)는 샘의 친구야, 그렇지 않아?
Yes, I am. / Yes, we are.

1253 너(희)는 지미의 친구가 아니야, 그렇지?
No, I'm not. / No, we aren't.
No, we're not.

1254 너(희)는 성미가 급하지 않아, 그렇지?
No, I'm not. / No, we aren't.
No, we're not.

1255 너(희)는 피아노를 쳐, 그렇지 않아?
Yes, I do. / Yes, we do.

1256 너(희)는 비 오는 날씨를 좋아하지 않아, 그렇지?
Yes, I do. / Yes, we do.

1257 너(희)는 어제 기분이 좋지 않았어, 그렇지?
No, I didn't. / No, we didn't.

1258 너(희)는 어젯밤 내게 이메일을 보냈어, 그렇지 않아?
Yes, I did. / Yes, we did.

1259 너(희)는 나랑 하이킹 갈 수 없어, 그렇지?
Yes, I can. / Yes, we can.

1260 너(희)는 하루 종일 기타를 칠 수 있어, 그렇지 않아?
No, I can't. / No, we can't.

1261 세라와 빌리는 좋은 친구야, 그렇지 않아?
No, they aren't. / No, they're not.

1262 세라와 빌리는 학교에 있지 않아, 그렇지?
Yes, they are.

1263 세라와 빌리는 멋져, 그렇지 않아?
No, they aren't. / No, they're not.

1264 세라와 빌리는 예의 없지, 그렇지?
Yes, they are.

1265 세라와 빌리는 그 비밀을 알고 있어, 그렇지 않아?
No, they don't.

1266 세라와 빌리는 탄산음료를 좋아하지 않아, 그렇지?
Yes, they do.

1267 세라와 빌리는 재미있게 놀지 않았어, 그렇지?
Yes, they did.

1268 세라와 빌리는 영화보러 갔어, 그렇지 않아?
No, they didn't.

1269 세라와 빌리는 이걸 기억할 수 있어, 그렇지 않아?
No, they can't.

1270 세라와 빌리는 서울을 떠나지 않았어, 그렇지?
Yes, they did.

Practice45

1271 What
1272 Where
1273 Who
1274 When
1275 Whose
1276 What
1277 Why
1278 Whose
1279 When
1280 Who

Practice46

1281 How can I find a convenience store?
제가 편의점을 어떻게 찾을 수 있을까요?
= 편의점 어디에요?

1282 How tall are Tom and his father?
톰과 그의 아버지는 키가 얼마야?

1283 How many days are there in a week?
일주일은 며칠이지?

1284 How long do you take a nap?
너는 낮잠 얼마나 자?

1285 How many pencils are there in your bag?
네 가방에 펜 몇 개 있어?

1286 How was your trip to the mountain?
산(의로의) 여행은 어땠어?

1287 How much are those onions?
저 양파(들)는 얼마에요?

1288 How far is the bus station from here?
여기에서 버스정류장까지는 얼마나 되죠?

1289 How much time do you need?

시간이 얼마나 필요해?

1290 How did he know the truth?

걔가 그 사실을 어떻게 알았지?

Practice47

1291	What	1296	Which
1292	What	1297	What
1293	Which	1298	What
1294	Which	1299	Which
1295	What	1300	What

Practice48

1301	1음절	[smɔːl]
1302	2음절	[táɪərd]
1303	3음절	[dífɪkəlt]
1304	1음절	[jʌŋ]
1305	1음절	[seɪf]
1306	2음절	[hévi]
1307	1음절	[laʊd]
1308	2음절	[féɪməs]
1309	3음절	[ətræktɪv]
1310	2음절	[rédi]
1311	1음절	[símpl]
1312	1음절	[wɔːrm]
1313	3음절	[nætʃərəl]
1314	3음절	[kʌmfərtəbl]
1315	2음절	[júːsfəl]
1316	1음절	[haɪ]
1317	1음절	[hɑt]
1318	3음절	[déɪndʒərəs]
1319	1음절	[maɪld]
1320	1음절	[tʌf]
1321	2음절	[kwáɪət]
1322	3음절	[impɔ́ːrtənt]
1323	2음절	[hǽnsəm]
1324	1음절	[kliːn]
1325	2음절	[nɔ́ɪzi]
1326	1음절	[wet]
1327	2음절	[fʌ́ni]
1328	2음절	[spéʃəl]
1329	3음절	[wʌ́ndərfəl]
1330	1음절	[lɑːrdʒ]

Practice49

1331	cuter
1332	colder
1333	more popular
1334	more beautifully
1335	more fluently
1336	the richest
1337	harder
1338	the best
1339	the most foolish
1340	older

Practice 50

1341 You are tall.
1342 I am taller than you.
1343 You are taller than him/he.
1344 He is taller than her/she.
1345 Your book is heavy.
1346 My book is heavier than yours.
1347 Your book is heavier than his.
1348 His book is heavier than hers.
1349 Her book is the heaviest.
1350 Daejeon is large.
1351 Daegu is larger than Daejeon.
1352 Busan is larger than Daegu.
1353 Seoul is larger than Busan.
1354 Seoul is the largest in Korea.
1355 Ryan is handsome.
1356 June is more handsome than Ryan.
1357 Tim is more handsome than June.
1358 Tim is the most handsome boy.
1359 Sally is good.
1360 David is better than Sally.
1361 Andy is better than David.
1362 Andy is the best.
1363 Horror movies are interesting.
1364 Action movies are more interesting than horror movies.
1365 Comedy movies are more interesting than action movies.
1366 Comedy movies are the most interesting.
1367 Jenny's voice is clear.
1368 Sam's voice is clearer than Jenny's.
1369 David's voice is clearer than Sam's.
1370 David's voice is the clearest.
1371 Emma is a pretty girl.
1372 Jessica is prettier than Emma.
1373 Ashley is prettier than Jessica.
1374 Ashley is the prettiest.
1375 Mr.Kim learns English quickly.
1376 Teenagers learn English more quickly than Mr.Kim.
1377 Children learn English more quickly than teenagers.
1378 Children learn English the most quickly.
1379 Question number 1 is easy.
1380 Question number 2 is easier than number 1.
1381 Question number 3 is easier than number 2.
1382 Question number 3 is the easiest.
1383 My father is older than me/I.
1384 My grandmother is older than my father.
1385 My grandfather is older than my grandmother.
1386 My grandfather is the oldest.

🐻 Practice51

1387 It was cool yesterday.
1388 It is rainy.
1389 It is fall(autumn).
1390 It is a foggy day.
1391 It is freezing outside.
1392 It will be cloudy tomorrow.
1393 It was too hot.
1394 It was winter.
1395 It may be snowy.
1396 I like a snowy day.
1397 It will be warm tomorrow.
1398 It is sunny.
1399 It is hot and humid in summer.
1400 It is windy in fall(autumn).

🐻 Practice52

1401 thirty-one
1402 eight hundred thirty-two
1403 nine hundred (and) one
1404 two thousand (and) forty-six
1405 one thousand eight hundred (and) forty-one
1406 thirty-six thousand seven hundred eight-five
1407 seventy-four thousand nine hundred (and) one
1408 seven hundred forty-nine thousand (and) thirty-four
1409 five hundred ninety thousand three hundred (and) eighty-five
1410 one million six hundred (and) seventy thousand
1411 five million thirty thousand two hundred (and) one
1412 eighty-four million nine hundred one thousand (and) two hundred
1413 fourteen million two hundred (and) thirteen
1414 eight hundred ninety-one million fifty thousand seven hundred (and) seventeen
1415 four hundred million three hundred seventy-six thousand nine hundred (and) twenty-four

🐻 Practice53

1416 third
1417 seventh
1418 fifth
1419 fourth
1420 second
1421 first
1422 eighth
1423 ninth

1424 sixth
1425 second
1426 fourteenth
1427 one hundred-first
1428 twenty-second
1429 tenth
1430 one hundredth

Practice 54

1431 I met him twice.
1432 She brushes her teeth three times a day.
1433 Her hair is three times longer than mine.
1434 I take a shower once a day.
1435 I do exercise three or four times a week.
1436 I go to work five times a week.
1437 Sam called me many times.
1438 The brand new battery is four times more durable than the old one.
1439 We go shopping twice a month.
1440 They save money twelve times a year.

Practice 55

1441 point seven (= zero point seven)
1442 one and a half (= one and one half)
1443 three point five
1444 three fifths
1445 five point seven five
1446 eleven point zero five
 (= eleven point o five)
1447 nine tenths
1448 six and one third
1449 twelve point three six
1450 thirty five one hundredths
1451 point nine four five
 (= zero point nine four five)
1452 three point one four
1453 seven and three fourths
 (= seven and three quarters)
1454 one point three four seven
1455 sixty three point six zero
 (= sixty three point six o)

Practice 56

1456 twenty-five thousand won
1457 fifty dollars (and) twenty-five cents
1458 one million eight hundred thousand won
1459 eight hundred million won

1460	sixty thousand two hundred thirty dollars (and) eighty-nine cents		1477	four forty-five (= fifteen to five = a quarter to five)
1461	one hundred five dollars (and) twenty cents		1478	three thirty (= half past/after three)
1462	four hundred fifty thousand won		1479	eight ten (= ten past/after eight)
1463	one hundred eighty-nine dollars		1480	eleven thirty-five
1464	thirty-four million won		1481	seven forty-three
1465	two hundred eighty-nine thousand four hunderd won		1482	ten twenty (= twenty past/after ten)
1466	thirty-nine dollars (and) ninety -nine cents		1483	nine-o-five (= five past/after nine)
1467	one million sixty-two thousand won		1484	five o'clock
1468	one thousand two hundred ninety-nine dollars		1485	two ten (= ten past/after two)

🐼 Practice 58

1486	May twenty-fifth
1487	March first
1488	December thirty-first
1489	June sixth
1490	nineteen eighty
1491	February fourteenth
1492	October ninth
1493	nineteen ninety-eight
1494	two thousand nine
1495	nineteen eighteen
1496	April fifth
1497	August fifteenth
1498	September twenty-second
1499	May twenty-seventh
1500	July fourteenth

1469 eighty-nine dollars (and) fifty cents
1470 fifteen dollars (and) thirty-nine cents.

🐼 Practice 57

1471 twelve-o-nine (= nine past/after twelve)
1472 five-o-five (= five past/after five)
1473 nine fifty (= ten to ten)
1474 seven forty-five (= fifteen to eight = a quarter to eight)
1475 one fifty-eight (= two to two)
1476 three fifteen (= fifteen past/after three = a quarter past/after three)